Ambushed in CHURCH?

Denny Harris

TEACH Services, Inc.
PUBLISHING
www.TEACHServices.com • (800) 367-1844

World rights reserved. This book or any portion thereof may not be copied or reproduced in any form or manner whatever, except as provided by law, without the written permission of the publisher, except by a reviewer who may quote brief passages in a review.

The author assumes full responsibility for the accuracy of all facts and quotations as cited in this book. The opinions expressed in this book are the author's personal views and interpretations, and do not necessarily reflect those of the publisher.

This book is provided with the understanding that the publisher is not engaged in giving spiritual, legal, medical, or other professional advice. If authoritative advice is needed, the reader should seek the counsel of a competent professional.

Copyright © 2015 Denny Harris

Copyright © 2015 TEACH Services, Inc.

ISBN-13: 978-1-4796-0594-1 (Paperback)

ISBN-13: 978-1-4796-0595-8 (ePub)

ISBN-13: 978-1-4796-0596-5 (Mobi)

Library of Congress Control Number: 2015916075

Published by

I dedicate this book to everyone that will take the time to read it and study the Word of God to see if these things are so.

ACKNOWLEDGMENT

I appreciate so much the work my wife Sandy did in deciphering and typing my scribbled manuscript. She's the best.

I am so very grateful to my daughter-in-law Kim Harris for her professional work of editing this book. She was a huge help in pulling it all together.

I also want to make known that I have the three greatest sons who gave us three great daughter-in-laws and the six greatest grandchildren in the world!

INTRODUCTION

As you read this book take your Bible and prayerfully follow the scriptures that are referenced. These scriptures are the Word of God. The magnitude of what Christ has done and continues to do for us is incomprehensible. Yet the plan of salvation is simple enough for a child to understand. Knowing Christ and trusting in His Word makes it easy to be saved. Without this knowledge the devil makes it easy to be lost through his work of deception.

    I have written this book to share the good news of salvation and also to expose the two greatest deceptions the devil has used for centuries to ambush the Christian church. I sense an urgency to write these pages because salvation is not like horseshoes; to be almost saved is to be entirely lost. I also have a special interest in my fellow veterans who have given so much for our country. You guys know about enemy fire and ambushes. I've shared a few of my experiences but spared you the details as my focus is on making known the truth found in God's word. So let's hit it!

CHAPTER I

The night was extremely hot. The rounds were incoming. Our bunker was taking direct hits and being blown apart. With the explosions, I heard the screams of pain, saw the blood, felt the helplessness. I was standing in a sea of chaos, a sea of death and dying. Then everything went blank as my mind started shutting down, but my body kept on going. One thought filled my mind and permeated my very being. I want to go home! I want to go home!

Home. How well I remember as a boy sitting on our front porch in the summer evenings. We didn't have television then; we had neighbors. The neighbors would be gathered around, visiting after work. We played horseshoes until dark, and then we would talk and listen to the whippoorwills singing their evening songs. Down at the pond the peepers would join the choir, doing their part. I loved to watch the sky light up with fireflies and listen to the stories being told.

Ambushed in CHURCH?

Then suddenly my life turned upside down. Drafted into the US Army at age 19, I was moved from the hills of Vermont to the Mekong Delta of South Vietnam. I became a combat medic. I requested non-combatant status; however, I was not a conscientious objector. I was convicted of my obligation to serve my country, but I also held to my belief that I should not take a life. I realized that in order to keep America free, some wars couldn't be avoided. As a combat medic I was there because I loved my country and wanted to do what I could to help save lives. Because of my non-combatant status, I was ridiculed, berated, and even threatened for refusing to carry a weapon.

> **Then one day word came down that tonight our company would be overrun. It was the Tet Offensive of 1968.**

Then one day word came down that tonight our company would be overrun. It was the Tet Offensive of 1968. The men were armed with all the weapons they could strap on. We had worked steadily all day filling sandbags and they were stacked high. As darkness began to fall, fears began to rise. The red lines of tracer bullets stretched from sky to jungle as gunships circled overhead. The men asked me to pray for them. They knew prayer was my weapon of choice. Men? Frightened boys, they were, just out of high school, but braver, truer, stronger than perhaps a lot of the politicians responsible for war.

However, war comes with a price tag. Imprinted somewhere on the walls of my mind are the screams

Chapter I

of wounded and dying that some of you can't hear, the blood and tears that some of you can't see, scenes that time cannot erase. Yes, Vietnam was a crazy place, not only for the physical aspect of the war but the psychological and emotional, as well. Bullets and blood mixed with drugs and fear. Anger and confusion created mega doses of adrenalin followed by tremendous fatigue. The excitement and joy of youth turned into hardness and scars. Beautiful sunrises and sunsets; and yet death hangs in the air. One minute I am sleeping, the next running for my life. One minute I'm asked to pray, the next I'm looking down the barrel of an M16, threatened for my faith.

I think you can relate, friend, because I know there are battles to be fought in your own life. Trauma, grief, pain, guilt, anger—touch the lives of each of us. Why is it so? Why is life so hard? Because we are living in a world that is a war zone. We have been overrun by Satan, and the battle is ultimately for your soul. However, be assured, there is a God in heaven who loves even you. He understands because He's been here once. He was a long way from home as He hung on that cross, but it was for you He came. For you He died. And for you He's coming again.

Perhaps it was so I could better relate to others that God allowed me to live and work the past 45 years on very limited amounts of sleep, walking the floors at night and working during the day, too often with virtually no sleep at all. At first it was the nightmares and then it became fear of the nightmares. I beat on myself and on the walls. I prayed. I cried. At the time, I had never heard of PTSD. Where was God when I needed Him?

Perhaps you have asked that same question. Only you know what you've been through or are going through, but to make it a fair question, I would have to ask: *Where was God when His Son needed Him at Calvary?* If you listen you can hear Jesus' agonizing cry, echoing down through the ages, "My God! My God! Why have you forsaken me?" (Matt. 27:46).

He was there. Think of the Father as He hears that cry; to see His Son tortured and hung up naked on a Roman cross, to be there with the power at His fingertips to cut those soldiers down and save His Son; to be there, yet unable to do a thing, because this was the plan. This was the plan, decided on before the foundation of the world was laid out: that should sin enter, the Creator of mankind would enter our world with an MOS (mission of assignment) to rescue every POW from hell. That's what this world has become, hasn't it? With the suffering, starvation, abuse, murder, addiction, terrorism, theft, disease, human trafficking, and natural disasters. As Merle Haggard sang, "Jesus, take a hold and lead us through!"

In order to lead us through, to make the rescue a success, the whole operation has to come together at the right time. It has three parts. First, God had to get into our arena and become one of us. He did this through the incarnation, the King of kings born of Mary in a stable. The Bible says of Him:

Chapter I

His name shall be Immanuel, meaning God with us (Matt. 1:23). He lived as we do with the same kind of feelings: hunger, pain, temptation, loneliness, homelessness. "A man of sorrows, and acquainted with grief" (Isa. 53:3).

So He was here. But He had to do more than just live here; He had to live here without sin. It's a natural law that God and sin cannot co-exist. Remember, this is God with us, but we are sinners, all of us. The Bible says: "For all have sinned, and come short of the glory of God" (Rom. 3:23). Also, Romans 6:23 says, "The wages of sin is death." But Jesus Christ never sinned, therefore He could not die! Only one without sin could for sin atone, but He without sin could not die. Do you see the trip wire here? The booby trap? The enemy, Satan, knew this. He thought he had us all locked in with the key thrown away, but he never really understood the plan.

The second part of the plan is Christ's sacrifice. In the Old Testament, the sacrificial lamb had to be without spot or blemish; then symbolically, the sins of the people were placed upon it and the lamb was killed. Jesus was the Lamb of God without blemish (sin). He could die only after taking your sins and mine upon Himself. In fact, the Bible says, He who knew no sin became sin for us (2 Cor. 5:21). Only then could He for sin atone. Now we can read the rest of the story. Yes, "the wages of sin is death; but the gift of God is eternal life through Jesus Christ our Lord" (Rom. 6:23).

I'm speaking of the Creator, the God of Heaven. John 1:1–3 explains: "In the beginning was the Word,

Ambushed in CHURCH?

and the Word was with God, and the Word was God. ... All things were made by Him; and without Him was not anything made that was made. And the Word became flesh, and dwelt among us" (John 1:1-3, 14). Here Christ is referred to as the Word. Your Creator, dear friend, is your Redeemer.

This reminds me of a man I once met. A patrol of Marines somehow got off course and ended up north of the DMZ (demilitarized zone) without realizing it. By accident they stumbled onto a North Vietnamese camp where several American soldiers were being held prisoner. The Vietnamese were taken by surprise and started running. The Marines found the Americans in bamboo cages that had been placed in water where bloodsuckers were gradually taking their lives. One of these men was almost left for dead. He was so weak he could not speak, but a Marine saw a flicker of life, so he picked this man up and carried him on his back. As they were running to the LZ (landing zone) for a chopper pick up, the Vietnamese had come back and were chasing them. This man on the Marines back was shot. The bullet went through his back and into the Marine. The Marine was killed, but I had the privilege of shaking the hand of the man he saved.

My friend, I'm talking about real stuff.
The Marine of Heaven has gone past the DMZ,
not by mistake, but purposely,
to bring you home.

Chapter I

My friend, I'm talking about real stuff. The Marine of Heaven has gone past the DMZ, not by mistake, but purposely, to bring you home. He died that you might live. Just now He sees that flicker of hope in you, so don't give up! Hold on! We're heading for the LZ.

Jesus Christ did not stay dead. There was a resurrection and with that resurrection came a promise kept. Christ Himself is going to make the pick-up. His tour of duty is not complete until He returns for you.

Maybe your wounds go deep. Maybe your country has forgotten you. Maybe you've lost your family, your lover, or your friends. Don't give up! There's a medevac waiting at the LZ with the Great Physician on board to heal those wounds.

Remember the plan? The plan was made for you. The first two steps have already been initiated. Jesus entered our arena, became one with us, carried your cross up Heartbreak Hill and gave His life for yours. Now, the third part of this great plan has to come together. That's your part, friend. It's simply your choice. The hard part is over. Jesus did it all. However, don't worry; He won't take you home if you don't want to go. When God created mankind He gave us a mind capable to choose. Unlike His adversary, the devil, the Lord forces no one to do what he doesn't want to do. Satan forces. When he gets a person on drugs or alcohol, for example, they become addicted, forced to continue in the habit. He thought he could force the Lord Jesus to remain in that tomb. He had a large stone rolled in front of the entrance, set up Roman soldiers to guard it, and seal it off. But He who broke the chains of death has the power to set you free. John 8:36 says: "If the Son shall make you free, you shall be free indeed!" The reason the term "if" is used in this verse is because it is your choice. If you want to be free, if you choose to be saved, if you want to go home, then there's a way. The God of Heaven has provided a way out of here. You simply must believe in Him enough to put all your weight on His back, trusting Him completely with your life.

I said the hard part is over; yet ironically, some find it hard to trust the One who gives and sustains their every heartbeat. There's only one reason for this lack of trust problem: We do not know Him. There are those who profess to be Christians that have the same problem. They think if they can overcome the enemy on every detail it will bring them up to God, so they struggle to make it on their own. They do not know Him. Knowing Him is the hinge on which the door to life swings open. The Bible says: "And this is life eternal, that they might know Thee, the only true God, and Jesus Christ whom Thou has sent" (John 17:3).

Who is this Jesus that the Bible calls King of kings and Lord of lords? Who is He that condescended to step from the glories of heaven to the stable manger in Bethlehem? Who is this Commander of the armies of heaven that came to His own people and had to run for His life? Who is this Creator that formed you and me from the dust and then died so that, after we blew it, He could re-create us in His image? He is the one that put the song in the sparrow. He is the one who paints the colors of the sunsets and

Chapter I

who dresses the flowers in such beautiful attire and sends out their perfumes for us to enjoy. He is the one who lets the eagle soar from lofty mountains to the sea. He is the one who freely gives us the bubbling streams and the air we breathe. He is the one who feeds the deer and sends the sunshine and rain. Just look at nature and what is seen from the microscope to the telescope. His creation is beyond imagination. We see His love in the innocent tender heart of a child. Looking through that scope we see ourselves standing in the shadow of a cross. Who is He? "You shall call His name Jesus, for He shall save His people from their sins" (Matt. 1:21).

Now, maybe you know what loneliness is all about, that feeling that there is no one to care if you're hungry or cold, that there is no one to care if you have no money or friends, that there is no one to hold or share your feelings with. My comrade, you are not out there alone. There is a God in Heaven who knows where you are and where you've been. He knows about loneliness. When it was all coming down on Him, just before His crucifixion, all His friends deserted Him. He died alone. But our salvation is sure.

The fourth chapter of Matthew tells us Jesus went into the wilderness alone, but the enemy was already there waiting for Him. After Jesus had eaten nothing for forty days, Satan came to Him and tempted Him to turn the stones into bread. The devil knows when and where to hit. If you had not eaten for forty days and you had the power to turn the stones into bread, would you? Jesus didn't because we can't.

Ambushed in CHURCH?

He had become one with us. He knew what hunger was. There in that wilderness of temptation the devil offered the Lord the world if He would simply bow down to him. Wow! Not only is the earth the Lord's, but He created it, and to Him every knee will one day bow. Satan is still on this theme of trying to receive the worship that is rightly God's alone. He said in Isaiah 14: 14, "I will ascend above the heights of the clouds; I will be like the Most High."

In Vietnam, I had a C.O. (Commanding Officer) whose character reminds me of Christ's character. Our C.O. of Delta Company, 9th Infantry, was replaced by a doctor who had been drafted. He wanted to go home as badly as I did, but as he took up his duty as C.O. there was quite a change for us. This man rolled up his sleeves, got down in the dirt, and worked with us. As a Captain he could have yelled orders; instead he treated his men with respect. He was dedicated to saving lives, and his gentle character was worthy of our obedience. It was a good feeling to do what he asked.

Although Jesus Christ was fully God, He came down to our level and became fully man, fully worthy of our love, honor, and devotion. Would you like to get to know the One who died for you? Would you choose to put your hand in His and say: "Yes, Lord, I admit it. I'm a sinner and deserve the wages, but I accept your death for me." You can go to your knees and meet this Jesus, right there in your living room, bedroom, basement, under the bridge, on the street, in the woods, wherever you are. Tell Him, "I'm sorry for my sin. Please forgive me, Lord. Your death will

Chapter I

no longer be in vain for me. I accept Your gift of life eternal. I choose to spend time with You and in Your word to get to know You as my friend and Savior. I choose to go home." If you so choose, prepare for battle, because you will come under enemy fire. The devil will try anything to hold you in the prison house of sin and slavery; but when Jesus says, "Follow Me," He will take you through and carry you when needed, and you will have a peace that passes understanding.

The plan of salvation is far more than what meets the eye. When this plan was put into action, this God of ours took the chance of losing everything. If He failed in His mission here by committing as much as one wrong act or thought, He could never again be restored to heaven, but would be lost with His people. This is a mystery that we, in our finite minds, cannot understand. The Bible refers to it as the "mystery of godliness." Think about it! Why would an all knowing, all powerful God give up all of heaven to save that which was already lost: you and me? A mystery indeed! Truly: "The love of God is greater far than we can ever understand. It goes beyond the highest star and reaches to the lowest hell."

This God of ours stood silent while men spit in His face, mocked Him, beat Him, whipped Him, and nailed Him to a tree. When He came into Jerusalem, He stopped and wept for His people, the vast majority of whom had rejected Him. "Neither is there salvation in any other: for there is none other name under heaven given among men, whereby we must be saved" (Acts 4:12). And they had rejected Him.

Ambushed in CHURCH?

Religious leaders and all! Well, not all. Some believed He was who He said He was. Some had been touched by the hand of God and were healed. Blind eyes had been opened. Dead had been raised to life. Sins had been forgiven. Would you be touched by the Hand of God? Or would you, too, reject this God of love?

Among those pictures imprinted on the walls of my mind comes to view a night-long battle in which we were caught in a crossfire. Bit by bit our shelter of sand bags was being blown away. There was no place to run. All night I held on to the only thing there was left for me to hold onto—and the only thing I needed—the Hand of God. With thousands of pieces of shrapnel constantly flying in every direction I was not hit, because He was holding me. Holding me in His arms of love under His protective care. That's what He did for me many times over.

I said I wanted to talk straight to your heart, so listen, my friend: the rounds are incoming.

I said I wanted to talk straight to your heart, so listen, my friend: the rounds are incoming. You are caught in the crossfire of the greatest battle ever fought. The battle is for your own soul! But it's almost over. The shelter we thought we had in this world is all but blown away. Our security of jobs and money lost in depression and recession. Taxes have chiseled away our farms and homes. The politicians have plans for the nation's recovery, but these fail and fold like the bags of sand. We're not safe in our houses; they're broken into. Murder, rape, robbery is everywhere.

Chapter I

People are living in constant fear. Evolutionists still teach about the progress of man to a higher order of being, while just the opposite is true. Yes, knowledge increases on one hand, but all about us we see the regression of mankind as generations of sin result in lower and baser standards of life.

A great cry is echoing around the world. It's a cry for peace, but I hear the rumble of war. The Bible says in 1 Thessalonians 5:3: "When they say, peace and safety; then sudden destruction comes upon them." Where are you going to run to? There's only one safe place, friend: right into the arms of Jesus.

You ask, "But how can I trust Someone I can't even see or hear? And heaven? I've never been there! I don't know what heaven's like. This world has been my home. I'm familiar with the sights and sounds and people here. I know my way around here. I don't want any more foreign lands."

Friend, I ask you to take a look around. Do you like what you see and hear in this world? Do you hear the babies cry as they starve to death? Do you see the torture chambers and feel the pain inflicted by man to man? Do you see the slaughter of Christians just because they're Christian? Did you know every two minutes a child is sexually abused? Do you see the turmoil in this world? Threats of war on every hand: Iran, North Korea, Russia, Afghanistan, Iraq. People die here every second. We're living on death row. If we put our trust in this world we have no hope. We'll be shot in the back for sure.

When Christ was here on earth the people watched

Ambushed in CHURCH?

Him heal the sick and raise the dead. They heard Him speak in person. Yet the majority rejected Him. So if seeing and hearing didn't work for many then, would it be any different now? Not likely. However, the answer is faith! The Bible says, "Now faith is the substance of things hoped for; the evidence of things not seen" (Heb. 11:1). It also says "The just shall live by faith" (Rom. 1:17).

In the process of obtaining my bachelor's degree in religion I had the opportunity to study the teachings of various religious denominations. It's astounding to realize that multitudes have been led to believe a lie right in church. However, it makes sense that the enemy of God would infiltrate the church. Where God's people congregate would be the most likely yet most unexpected place for an ambush.

For now in speaking to the Pharisees Jesus said in John 8:44 that "[the devil] is a liar, and the father of it." As I said earlier, the greatest battle ever fought is the battle for your soul; the great deceiver's war strategy can be very subtle. He has masterminded a plan that catches millions of innocent people within the churches in the name of religion.

The Lord Jesus loves people with all of His heart and all of heaven. When the whip tore and ripped His flesh and the nails pierced through His hands and feet and He was hanging on that cross, it was for you, my friend and comrade. Saint or sinner, lost or found, He could not love you any more than He does. His children are most precious to Him, and we find His children all over this world, from all different

Chapter I

cultures and backgrounds, from all different faiths and denominations. Those who sincerely proclaim the name of Jesus and choose to follow Him are adopted into the family of God. Ephesians 1:4–5 says: "According as he hath chosen us in him before the foundation of the world, that we should be holy and without blame before him in love: Having predestinated us unto the adoption of children by Jesus Christ to himself, according to the good pleasure of His will." He chose us, and predestinated us to be saved based on our choice to believe and follow Him. Therefore what I have to say here is not directed to individuals, for we are all sinners; but rather to false doctrines and teachings. To expose the lie.

As I enter into the topics of the two greatest deceptions the world has ever seen, please understand I have no desire to hurt or offend anyone. It's just my sincere desire to make the truth known, because the lives of precious souls are at stake for eternity. I only ask for your honesty and your earnest study, because truth will stand any investigation you can give it. Personally I would rather know the naked truth than a dressed up lie.

CHAPTER II

Isaiah 1:18 says, "Come now, and let us reason together." Our God is reasonable so let's just use the Bible and simple common sense.

The point man walks in front of the patrol. He must be very alert for there are many dangers in the path ahead. Jesus is our point man, but He knows what lies ahead. He says in Matthew 24:24, "For there shall arise false Christs, and false prophets, and shall show great signs and wonders, insomuch that if it were possible, they shall deceive the very elect." I'm not going to discuss the religions of the Buddhas and Mohammeds of the world. They are dead and the falsities of their teachings are obvious to the Christian.

I'm going to do some straight shooting now. The first great deception I will address is the very point that Christian churches exist. The purpose of worship.

Chapter II

I have always been amazed at what lengths so many Bible scholars will go to get around the fourth commandment of God's moral law. Most sincere Christians believe the Ten Commandments that were written in stone with God's own finger are still valid today, for God does not change. He is the same yesterday, today, and forever.

The breaking down of these Ten Commandments parallels the breaking down of the moral fabric of our society. Christians would agree with that. A Christian says it is wrong and it's sin to have other gods before us, to dishonor mother and father, to steal from our neighbor, to commit adultery, to kill, to bear false witness. Nine out of ten are upheld by the vast majority of Christians, but that fourth commandment seems to be a thorn in the side; thus many explanations are manufactured to get around a "thus saith the Lord." Let's begin by looking at the fourth commandment and then the most popular explanations.

Exodus 20:8–11 says:

Remember the Sabbath day to keep it holy. Six days shalt thou labor and do all thy work. But the seventh day is the Sabbath of the Lord thy God: in it thou shalt not do any work: thou, nor thy son, nor thy daughter, thy manservant, nor thy maidservant, nor thy cattle, nor thy stranger that is within thy gates: For in six days the Lord made heaven and earth, the sea, and all that in them is, and rested the seventh day: wherefore the Lord blessed the seventh day and hallowed it.

Ambushed in CHURCH?

You will notice the seventh day is the Sabbath of the Lord. That would be the Lord's Day, would it not? Mark 2:28 says, "Therefore the Son of man is Lord also of the Sabbath," therefore we certainly can't say from a Biblical standpoint that the first day, or Sunday, is the Lord's Day.

We also notice in the fourth commandment that the Lord Himself rested on the seventh day and blessed it and hallowed it. To hallow is to make holy. It's the only day of the week He made holy. To call another day holy doesn't make it so. You can call a BB gun an M-16, but it doesn't make it so. Likewise, you can call Sunday the Sabbath, but it doesn't make it so.

Another popular attempt to circumvent the fourth commandment is to say the Sabbath is a Jewish institution, meant only for the Jews. Let's be real and look to the Bible? Right after creating Adam and Eve, God instituted the Sabbath at the end of creation week. Let's read it in Genesis 2:1–3: "Thus the heavens and the earth were finished, and all the hosts of them. And on the seventh day God ended His work which He had made ... and God blessed the seventh day, and sanctified it: because that in it He had rested from all His works which He had created and made."

Sounds a lot like the fourth commandment, doesn't it? We notice in this passage that God sanctified the seventh day. To sanctify is to set apart for holy use. The Bible is very specific as to which day is blessed, hallowed, and sanctified.

Sadly, the nation chosen by God to be a light to the world had, by the time Jesus came to earth, become

Chapter II

very legalistic and had made up hundreds of laws of their own. They had made the Sabbath a heavy burden. For example, they could only turn to the right, only carry so much change in their pocket, only walk so far, could not help anyone in need, and much more. The list is very lengthy and tedious. Jesus tried to show them by word and by example that it was lawful to do good on the Sabbath day. "And he said unto them, what man shall there be among you, that shall have one sheep, and if it fall into a pit on the sabbath day, will he not lay hold on it, and lift it out? How much then is a man better than a sheep? Wherefore it is lawful to do well on the sabbath days" (Matt. 12:11–12).

The apostle Paul said in Galatians 3:13 that Christ has redeemed us from the curse of the law. Please note, Paul is referring to the curse the Jews had made of it and not the law itself. Otherwise he could not be in harmony with what he said elsewhere; for example, Romans 3:31 where he said, "Do we then make void the law through faith? God forbid!" In Romans 7:12 he said, "The law is holy, and the commandment holy, just, and good." And isn't that exactly what God is? Holy, just, and good? The law of God is a reflection of God's character.

Another false idea is the law was nailed to the cross according to Colossians 2:14–17. Keep in mind it's only the fourth commandment the popular religions want to nail. This passage in Colossians says the handwriting of ordinances (referring to the hand writing of Moses in regards to the Old Testament sacrificial systems) was nailed to the cross. The killing

Ambushed in CHURCH?

of animals, holy days, and Sabbath days were all a shadow of things to come. When Christ died on the cross, that whole system came to an end. There were special feast days, holy days, and sabbath days that pointed forward to Christ, but had nothing to do with the Ten Commandment law of God, written in stone with His own finger. If it did, the Bible would be contradicting itself.

Another thought some adhere to is the fact the calendar has been changed over the years. Thus it's believed by some that we don't actually know which day is the seventh day of the week. You can take days out, but morning always follows evening. For example, we find:

> As the centuries passed, the Julian calendar became more inaccurate. Because the calendar was incorrectly determining the date of Easter, Pope Gregory XIII reformed the calendar to match the solar year so that Easter would once again "fall upon the first Sunday after the first full moon on or after the Vernal equinox". Ten days were omitted from the calendar to bring the calendar back in line with the solstices, and Pope Gregory XIII decreed that the day following Thursday, October 4, 1582 would be Friday, October 15, 1582 and from then on the reformed Gregorian calendar would be used (Ancestor Search).

As you can see, the weekly cycle of 7 days can't be broken, one day follows another, Wednesday is

Chapter II

followed by Thursday, followed by Friday, etc. Even atheists adhere to a seven-day week.

Another concept is that Sunday is holy because it's the day we celebrate Christ's resurrection. Certainly if it weren't for the cross and the resurrection, we would have no hope. However, the Lord's Supper, or the Communion service, is what honors Christ's sacrifice, and baptism is symbolic of death to self, and resurrection to new life in Christ.

Nowhere in Scripture does Jesus change the sacredness of the Sabbath to another day. In fact, while He was here He gave us the example in Luke 4:16: "As His custom was, He went into the synagogue on the Sabbath day and stood up for to read." It's clear that being in church on the Sabbath day was customary for Him. This is what Jesus did. Thirty years after His resurrection, the apostle Paul was still doing the same thing. "But when they departed from Perga, they came to Antioch in Pisidia, and went into the synagogue on the Sabbath day, and sat down" (Acts 13:14).

We could go on, but friend, the Bible traces the Sabbath down through the ages from Genesis to Revelation. I worship the Lord on the seventh-day Sabbath because that's what Jesus did and He asks me to. He said in John 14:15, "If you love Me, keep My commandments." The fourth commandment does not begin with the word "forget" but rather with the word

> *The fourth commandment does not begin with the word "forget" but rather with the word "remember".*

"remember". I can't find in the New Testament or the Old Testament where He offers a ten-percent-off sale on His holy law. There are still ten.

But there's a reason why the fourth commandment is under attack and is one of the greatest deceptions of all time. I want to go back to something in that fourth commandment that I passed by, something that tells the why the Bible has so much to say on the subject of worship and the attempted change of God's law. First of all, I want to point out that the fourth commandment is the only one of the ten that tells us the name of God, His title, and His domain in which He rules. It says, "For in six days the Lord made heaven and earth, the sea and all that in them is." His name is "Lord." His title, indicated by the word *made*, is Creator. And finally, His domain is the heavens, the earth, and the sea, and everything that is in them. It's very important that we understand this before we move on, because this is what entitles Him to be worshipped. He alone is our God, our Creator, our Redeemer and Sustainer of life.

Revelation 14:7 says, "Worship Him that made heaven, and earth, and sea." Again we see the language of the fourth commandment. You see, Satan wanted worship for himself. He wanted to put himself in place of God. This is what he said in Isaiah 14:12–14: "How art thou fallen from heaven, O Lucifer, son of the morning! How art thou cut down to the ground, which did weaken the nations. For thou hast said in thine heart, I will ascend into heaven; I will exalt my throne above the stars of God. I will sit also upon the mount of the congregation, in the sides of the north.

Chapter II

I will ascend above the heights of the clouds; I will be like the Most High." As we can see, his plan is to usurp God's throne.

Let's look at how Satan masterminded the greatest deception the world has ever seen. The books of Daniel and Revelation expose him. If you read chapter 2 of the book of Daniel you will see in verse 1 that Nebuchadnezzar, king of Babylon, had a dream that troubled him greatly. But he couldn't recall it. All his wise men could not tell it or interpret it. But God showed Daniel the dream and the interpretation. So in verse 31, Daniel begins to tell the King what he saw. He saw a great image of a man whose head was of fine gold, his breast and arms of silver, his belly and thighs of brass, his legs of iron, and feet part iron and part clay. Then he saw a great stone strike the image and it broke the iron, clay, brass, silver and gold into pieces and blew it away. Then in verse 36 Daniel begins to tell the king the interpretation.

Take the time to read this story for yourself in Daniel, chapter 2, and you will see this amazing prophecy of the rise and fall of the four world empires, a prophecy verified to us by our history books. Verse 38 identifies Nebuchadnezzar's Babylon as the head of gold. Babylon is known as the golden empire, a wonder of the world. The next world empire that came on the scene was Medo-Persia. Babylon fell to the Medes and Persians in 539 B.C. Next on the scene was Greece, led by Alexander the Great, and represented by the belly and thighs of brass in the image. Medo-Persia fell in 331 B.C. The fourth

Ambushed in CHURCH?

world empire was the iron monarchy of Rome, represented by the legs of iron. Greece fell to Rome in 168 B.C.

History shows us that men like Napoleon, Hitler, and others tried to unite the world into another world empire, but like the feet of iron and clay, they couldn't mix. They failed. The prophecy says only four world empires. The next kingdom represented by the stone that blows the rest away is the kingdom of God, when Jesus, the Rock of Ages, comes again and sets up the Kingdom that shall never be destroyed. See verse 44.

Sometimes God repeats a prophecy and enlarges on it to give us a more clear understanding. We find this prophecy of world empires repeated in Daniel chapter 7, only this time God gives Daniel a vision of these empires represented by four beasts instead of four metals. In Daniel 7:1–7 he sees a lion, the king of beasts, representing the powerful kingdom of Babylon. The second beast he sees is a bear, representing Medo-Persia. The bear raises itself up on one side in verse five, indicating one side is stronger than the other. History shows that the Persians were the stronger of this dual kingdom of the Medes and Persians. The next beast Daniel sees is a leopard with four wings and four heads. Wings represent speed, and it was with great speed that Alexander the Great conqucred the world. He did it in ten years. Verse 6 also says this leopard had four heads. History tells us that after this great Grecian conqueror died at the age of thirty-three, the kingdom of Greece was divided between

Chapter II

his four generals: Cassander, Lysimachus, Ptolemy and Seleucus.

So far we've seen nothing in the realm of deception. These prophecies have come to pass and are recorded in the history books. By now I imagine that you are thinking, "What does this have to do with the subject of Sabbath worship?" Please watch carefully now and see what materializes out of the fourth beast.

Daniel 7:7 says this fourth beast is dreadful and terrible with great iron teeth and it has ten horns. You'll notice this parallels the fourth kingdom of Nebuchadnezzar's image in chapter 2. Remember the iron legs representing the kingdom of Rome? The ten horns parallel the feet with ten toes. These ten horns represent the ten major nations of Europe: Franks (France), Alemanni (Germany), Burgundians (Switzerland), Anglo-Saxons (Britain), Suevi (Portugal), Lombards (Italy), Visigoths (Spain), and the Vandals, Heruli, Ostrogoths, (Barbarian tribes). Rome was the world power from 168 B.C. to 476 A.D.

Now look what Daniel sees next in verse 8: "I considered the horns, and, behold, there came up among them another little horn, before whom there were three of the first horns plucked up by the roots; and, behold, in this horn were eyes like the eyes of man, and a mouth speaking great things." This little horn uproots three of the other horns. History tells us Rome utterly destroyed the Vandals, the Ostrogoths, and the Heruli. These nations no longer exist. But notice here in verse 8, this little horn has eyes like a man and a mouth speaking great things. Also

Ambushed in CHURCH?

notice this little horn is diverse or different from the ones before it. All the other nations were political, but this little horn we are soon to see is a religious power with the eyes and mouth of a man.

Read carefully Daniel 7:19–25. In verse 19 Daniel says, "I would know the truth of the fourth beast." And in verse 21, "The same horn made war with the saints." Then in verse 25, "He shall speak great words against the most High, and shall wear out the saints of the most High, and think to change times and laws." Remember in Isaiah 14:12–14 where Lucifer (Satan) said he would be like the most high? Satan's goal has always been to be worshipped as God.

History tells us that in the fourth century A.D. the Roman Emperor Constantine made a most clever political move to bring the two worlds together: paganism and Christianity. He supposedly became converted to Christianity. He had his whole army baptized. The problem is that when Constantine came into the church he brought with him many beliefs and practices he was accustomed to. Most significant of these was sun worship. "The devotion of Constantine was more peculiarly directed to the genius of the sun ... the sun was universally celebrated as the invisible guide and protector of Constantine" (Barry 291). To make a separation from the Jews there began a gradual transfer of the day of worship from the seventh day to the first day, or Sunday.

Pagan Rome has metamorphosed into Papal Rome,

This is a trip wire that catches the whole world off guard.

Chapter II

The Holy Roman Empire. Satan uses this religious power to receive worship to himself. This is a trip wire that catches the whole world off guard. Satan's long laid plan was now taking shape. He now entered the church. However, the apostle Paul said in 2 Thessalonians 2:7, "the mystery of iniquity doth already work." In verses 3–4 Paul said, "Let no man deceive you by any means." He said, "that man of sin will be revealed, the son of perdition; who opposeth and exalteth himself above all that is called God, or that is worshipped; so that he as God sitteth in the temple of God, shewing himself that he is God" (2 Thess. 2:3–4). Remember what we read in Isaiah 14:12–14? This is exactly what Lucifer said he would do.

In 321 A.D. Constantine declared Sunday a general "holiday" (Boak 432-3). By 538 A.D. a pope was set up as having the power and authority to make laws and change laws and whatever he decreed would be enforced by the state. Watch this: "The pope is of so great authority and power he can modify, explain, or interpret even divine laws" (Ferraris 29). "Hence the pope is crowned with a triple crown, as king of heaven, and of earth, and of the lower regions." (Ferraris 26).

Satan is a master of deception. It's my prayer that you, dear reader, are beginning to see the war strategy of the great counterfeiter as he uses men like Constantine and the

> **Watch this:**
> ***"The pope is of so great authority and power he can modify, explain, or interpret even divine laws"***
> *(Ferraris 29).*

popes to set up a system of worship that is antichrist, but in the name of Christ, and within the church.

In Daniel chapter 7 we read how that little horn would be different in nature from the kingdoms before it. "And he shall speak great words against the most High, and shall wear out the saints of the most High, and think to change times and laws; and they shall be given into his hand until a time and times and the dividing of time" (Dan. 7:25).

The record of history shows that from 538 A.D. when that pope took his throne a time of terrible persecution began. Those who would not bow to the pope and his demands were tortured, racked, burned at the stake, etc. It's estimated between 50,000,000 and 100,000,000 souls were martyred at the hands of the Church of Rome, all in the name of religion. This is known as the Dark Ages: dark because of persecution, but also dark because the people were not allowed to have or read the Bible. You can read about the terrible persecution of God's faithful people during those dark ages in books like Foxe's Book of Martyrs, or the History of the Waldensians. This papal power kept them in darkness, kept them away from the wonderful light of God's Word. The kings of the nations were in submission to the pope and carried out his dastardly deeds.

It's estimated between 50,000,000 and 100,000,000 souls were martyred at the hands of the Church of Rome, all in the name of religion.

Chapter II

In chapter 12 of the book of Revelation, God's church is represented by a pure woman. It says in verse 6 that she flees into the wilderness for 1260 days. Bible prophecy is completely accurate. Using the day-for-a-year principal found in Numbers 14:34 and Ezekiel 4:6 and elsewhere in Scripture, we find that a day equals a year, but only as it applies to prophetic time. Thus 1260 days would be 1260 years. The Jewish calendar had 30 days to a month, so the 42 months of Revelation 13:5 equals 1260 years, the time of Revelation 12:14 equals one year, the times would be two years, and the half time would be a half year. Three and a half years of thirty days to a month equals exactly 1260 years. This is the very same time frame used in Daniel 7:25 where it says the power would be given into the hand of that little horn for a time, times, and the dividing of time.

From the time the pope was put in power in 538 A.D. to 1798 A.D. was exactly 1260 years. What happened in 1798 A.D.? History tells us the French General Berthier marched into Rome and took the pope captive. He died in captivity, bringing an end to papal supremacy.

The Bible prophesies, history verifies, and I have got to tell it like it is to identify. I'm not condemning or speaking about individuals. There are many wonderful Christians in all denominations and throughout the Catholic Church. I am simply identifying a system of religion that Satan has used to deceive the masses. Although the 1260 years ended, the battle for your soul and the activity of that little horn has

Ambushed in CHURCH?

not. In Revelation 13:3 it tells us that this beast that was wounded to death, his deadly wound was healed and "all the world wondered after the beast." The fulfillment of this prophecy is astounding. Today we can see how this wound is healed as the Church of Rome is calling for all her children (all denominations) to come home to the mother church.

Just recently I watched on YouTube the most subtle, most deceptively convincing speech I've ever heard. A close friend of Pope Francis was addressing a group of Protestants. He spoke of Martin Luther, the great Protestant reformer, who, through Bible study, had come to realize that we are saved by grace alone. He said the protest is over; we, the Catholic Church, agree. We are all saved by grace alone. We are all one in Christ. We are all catholic [catholic means universal]. It's time the Protestants took back what they own: Catholicism.

If we are not aware that this is where Satan has set up his day of worship, Sunday in place of Saturday, we will be ambushed right in church. I'm telling you folks, the deception is most overwhelming if we don't know our Bible.

In the book of Revelation, chapter 14, verses 6 through 12, there are shown three angels carrying three last warning messages to this dying world. In the first angel's message is the call to worship God as Creator. It says in verses 6 and 7: "And I saw another angel flying in the midst of heaven, having the everlasting gospel to preach unto them that dwell on the earth, and to every nation, and kindred, and

Chapter II

tongue, and people, saying with a loud voice, 'Fear God, and give glory to Him; for the hour of His judgment is come: and worship Him that made heaven, and earth, and the sea, and the fountains of waters.'" And verse 12 says: "Here are they which keep the commandments of God, and the faith of Jesus."

The first angel's message is a call to worship God as Creator within the everlasting gospel because He made heaven, earth, sea; and also the hour of His judgment is come (Revelation 14:6). The message of the second angel in verse 8 is that Babylon is fallen, because she made all nations drink the wine of her fornication. Keep in mind that ancient Babylon fell way back in 539 B.C, so in Revelation it's talking about spiritual Babylon. The word Babylon comes from back when after the flood people began to build the tower of Babel to escape another flood. God stopped this building project by confusing their language. The people couldn't understand each other. This word "Babel" or "Babylon" means confusion.

Through the influence and deceptions of the papacy, the nations have committed spiritual fornication. Being intoxicated with her wine of deception, the nations hold her up in high esteem. When you consider the hundreds of different Christian denominations, most of them using the same Bible but teaching different doctrines, it results in confusion (Babylon) for the sincere seekers of truth.

Being intoxicated with her wine of deception, the nations hold her up in high esteem.

Ambushed in CHURCH?

In Revelation 17:2 the Bible speaks again about the nations being drunk with her wine. Notice the term her being used.

Remember in Revelation 12 it speaks of a woman that is persecuted. She represents the pure woman or church that had to flee and hide out for 1260 years.

However, the woman in Revelation 17 represents the apostate church. Let's look at her Revelation 17:4–6:

> And the woman was arrayed in purple and scarlet color, and decked with gold and precious stones and pearls, having a golden cup in her hand full of abomination and filthiness of her fornication. And upon her forehead was a name written: MYSTERY, BABYLON THE GREAT, THE MOTHER OF HARLOTS AND ABOMINATION OF THE EARTH. And I saw the woman drunken with the blood of the saints and with the blood of the martyrs of Jesus.

This is a church of great wealth, with a history of terrible persecution to God's faithful ones. You may have seen the Vatican with its stores of riches, or a priest drinking from a golden cup, or the purple and scarlet dress of the bishops and cardinals. These colors represent royalty.

Pope Francis is courting the world with humbleness and love, and he may well be very sincere; but the Bible is true, and the message of the third angel in Revelation 14:9 is a last warning message to the

Chapter II

world. It is a warning not to worship the beast or its image or receive its mark in the forehead or in the hand.

There is much more to study on this, but I must

> *The Bible is true, and the message of the third angel in Revelation 14:9 is a last warning message to the world.*

stay focused on my topic of how this all plays into the subject of worship, So let's trace this little horn of Daniel 7 over to Revelation.

In Revelation 13:1 the apostle John sees in vision a beast come up out of the sea. Beasts, we have found, symbolize nations, kings, and kingdoms as shown in Daniel 7:1-7 and 17. Now we need to identify what the sea symbolizes in this verse (Revelation 13:1) and we find the answer in Revelation 17:15. It says, "The waters which thou sawest, where the whore sitteth, are peoples, and multitudes, and nations, and tongues." This whore sits there within the populace of the European nations. She is called a whore because she commits spiritual fornication with the nations.

Ah, so this power arises out of a populated part of the world. It has ten horns like the one in Daniel, but notice this time the Bible expands a little further and says there are crowns on the horns. Why? It is because the nations of Europe had kings in power. We also notice in this verse the name of blasphemy on its head. To blaspheme is to stand in place of, or instead of, God. In the gospel of Matthew 9:2–3 Jesus was accused of blasphemy when He told the man his sins were forgiven. They knew only God can

Ambushed in CHURCH?

forgive sins, but Jesus was God in the flesh.

So I ask you, what man or system of religion on earth claims the power to forgive sins? It would be the one with the confessional, would it not? It is the one where millions go and confess their sins before the priest. Oh, what blasphemy! Christ alone can forgive our sins and to Him alone should we confess our sins. Read 1 John 1:9 and find that beautiful promise: "If we confess our sins He is faithful and just to forgive us our sins and to cleanse us from all unrighteousness."

In Revelation 13:2 John describes this beast as a composite of all four beasts of Daniel 7; but notice: it's the dragon that gives the beast its power, and seat, and great authority. Revelation 12:9 identifies the dragon as the devil and Satan. Papal Rome with its pope and cardinals are just a pawn in Satan's hands.

As we read Revelation 13 we find that it's all about worship. Verse 4 says they worshipped the dragon, and they worshipped the beast. Verse 5 says he was given a mouth speaking great things. Daniel 7:8 says that little horn comes up out of that fourth beast and in verse 25 it says he would think to change times and laws. Let's look at what the papacy did with God's law. They took out the second commandment that says not to make images or bow down to them, then they split the tenth one so they still end up with ten. Now you'll notice that the only commandment that has to do with time is the fourth. It was indeed the Church of Rome that changed the Sabbath of the Lord from the seventh day to the first, an act by

Chapter II

which they openly boast of. The Catholic catechism states very clearly that they (the Catholic Church) changed the solemnity of the seventh day to the first. Check it out for yourself.

As I stated earlier, there are many wonderful Christians in the Catholic Church, but the church system of religion is very pagan in nature, with all its images and relics that date back to Constantine. Some examples of topics that are not found in God's word are purgatory, the mass, transubstantiation, penance, hail Marys, blowing smoke over caskets, and so much more. This system of religion caused the great men of the reformation to stand up and tell the truth about salvation in Christ and His righteousness alone. Many of these men were killed, men like Tyndale, Huss, Jerome, and so many more. It is through this system of religion that Satan has exalted himself. By attempting to change God's law and setting up a false day of worship, Satan has obtained worship unto himself. Millions of sincere Christians today worship on Sunday, not realizing these things. We praise God for those great reformers that brought about the Protestant Reformation. However; one thing still remains: Sunday worship has come down to us through hundreds of years of tradition.

The vast majority of Protestants observe Sunday because of tradition, but with absolutely no Biblical support. Look at what The Catholic Record says: "The church is above the Bible, and transference of Sabbath observance from Saturday to Sunday is proof positive of that fact." In *Plain Talk about*

Ambushed in CHURCH?

Protestantism Louis Segun asserts, "The observance of Sunday by the Protestants is an homage they pay, in spite of themselves, to the authority of the Catholic Church." And in *The Catholic Universe Bulletin* we find, "The [Catholic] Church changed the observance of the Sabbath to Sunday by right of the divine, infallible authority given to her by her Founder, Jesus Christ. The Protestant claiming the Bible to be the only guide of faith has no warrant for observing Sunday. In this matter, the Seventh-day Adventist is the only consistent Protestant."

In a letter, C.F. Thomas, Chancellor of Cardinal Gibbons declares, "Of course the Catholic Church claims that the change was her act, and the act is a MARK of her ecclesiastical power and authority in religious matters."

And again,

> Our Church took pagan philosophy and made it the buckler of faith against the heathen. She took pagan Roman Pantheon, temple of all gods, and made it sacred to all martyrs: and so it stands to this day. She took THE PAGAN SUNDAY AND MADE IT THE CHRISTIAN SUNDAY. She took the pagan Easter and made it the feast we now celebrate (Catholic World).

But since Saturday--not Sunday--is specified in the Bible, isn't it curious that non-Catholics who profess to take their religion directly from the Bible and not from the church, observe Sunday instead

Chapter II

of Saturday? Yes, of course, it is inconsistent but this change was made about fifteen centuries before Protestantism was born, and by that time the custom was universally observed. They have continued the custom, even though it rests upon the authority of the Catholic Church and not upon an explicit text in the Bible. That observance remains as a reminder of the mother Church from which the non-Catholic sects broke away – like a boy running away from home but still carrying in his pocket a picture of his mother or a lock of her hair (O'Brien 473).

Please don't take my word for this information. You can research it and check it out for yourself. These are just a very few of many quotations from Catholic publications, many of which say the change of the Sabbath is their <u>mark of ecclesiastical authority</u>.

Here are what some main-line Protestant churches say:

- <u>BAPTISTS</u>: Dr. Edward T. Hiscox, author of the Baptist Manual said, ""There was and is a commandment to keep holy the Sabbath day, but that Sabbath day was not Sunday. It will be said, however, and with some show of triumph, that the Sabbath was transferred from the seventh to the first day of the week ... Where can the record of such a transaction be found? Not in the New Testament absolutely not.

    "To me it seems unaccountable that Jesus, during three years' intercourse with His disciples, often conversing with them upon the Sabbath question ... never alluded to any transference of the day; also, that during forty days of His resurrection life, no such thing was intimated.

"Of course, I quite well know that Sunday did come into use in early Christian history. ... But what a pity it comes branded with the mark of paganism, and christened with the name of the sun god, adopted and sanctioned by the papal apostasy, and bequeathed as a sacred legacy to Protestantism!"

- <u>CHURCH OF ENGLAND</u> (Episcopal): Sir William Domville: "Centuries of the Christian era passed away before Sunday was observed by the Christian Church as Sabbath. History does not furnish us with a single proof or indication that it was at any time so observed previous to the Sabbatical edict of Constantine in 321 A.D" (291).

- <u>PRESBYTERIANS:</u> "So some have tried to build the observance of Sunday upon Apostolic command, whereas the Apostles gave no command on the matter at all ... The truth is, so soon as we appeal to the litera scripta of the Bible, the Sabbatarians have the best of the argument." (qtd. in Christian at Work).

- <u>CONGREGATIONAL</u>: In *The Ten Commandments* Dr. R.W. Dale says, "It is quite clear that however rigidly or devotedly we may

Chapter II

spend Sunday, we are not keeping the Sabbath. The Sabbath was founded on a specific, divine command. We can plead no such command for the observance of Sunday ... there is not a single sentence in the New Testament to suggest that we incur any penalty by violating the supposed sanctity of Sunday." (106–7).

- LUTHERAN: "The observance of the Lord's day (Sunday) is founded not on any command of God, but on the authority of the Church" (*Augsburg Confession*).

- METHODIST: "It is true, there is no positive command for infant baptism. Nor is there any for keeping holy the first day of the week" (Binney 180–1).

If you feel like you've been duped or lied to, don't despair; Jesus finds us where we are and leads us on to further light. Many of these leaders have either forgotten or never knew how this all came about.

What is the mark of the beast? Obviously it is Sunday, but only when it is legislated by civil government do people receive it. The Bible even tells us where the mark is placed. Speaking of the beast power, Revelation 13:16 says: "And he causeth all, both small and great, rich and poor, free and bond, to receive a mark in their right hand or in their foreheads." Verse 17 says no one will be able to buy or sell unless he has that mark.

Ambushed in CHURCH?

Notice the mark is in <u>the forehead</u>. The forehead is the part of the brain (frontal lobe) where we think and make choices. The hand symbolizes carrying out those decisions and choices. It's not a physical mark we can see, but a choice we make in our minds and hearts. Compare this to Revelation 7:3 where it says God's servants are sealed in <u>their foreheads</u>. Remember God's seal is the Sabbath, the commandment with His name and title on it. There it is! The question is: will you choose the mark of the beast or the seal of God? Where will you stand, my friend?

> *There it is!*
> *The question is: will you choose the mark of the beast or the seal of God?*
> *Where will you stand, my friend?*

The fourth commandment says to remember the Sabbath day to keep it holy, referring back to Genesis 2:3 in honor of God's creation. This commandment is repeated in Deuteronomy 5:15 where again God says to remember. In this text the Lord is referring to Israel's deliverance from Egyptian bondage, symbolic of Christ's delivering us from the bondage of sin. Take some time to read it for yourself.

It's quite clear that the Sabbath is both a memorial of creation and redemption. If we cannot stand on these two doctrines we really have nothing to stand on. These are foundational to Christianity. What a God we have! We belong to our heavenly Father through creation and through redemption. At the end of the day, everyone will have made a stand either on the Word of God or on the word of the deceiver.

Chapter II

The enforcement of worship is nothing new. We've touched on what happened during the 1260 years of the Dark Ages. However, let's go back for a moment to the book of Daniel, and look at the great ecumenical movement recorded in chapter 3.

Nebuchadnezzar wasn't satisfied being just the head of gold depicted in the image of his vision in chapter 2. It says in Daniel 3:1 that he made an image of gold sixty cubits high and six cubits wide. That's nearly 100 feet high. Then he sent out the order in verse 2 for everyone to come and gather before this image, even all the rulers of provinces.

Now look at the enforcement of worship to an image with the attachment of a death decree. Daniel 3:4–6: "Then an herald cried aloud, To you it is commanded, O people, nations, and languages, That at what time ye hear the sound of the cornet, flute, harp, sackbut, psaltery, dulcimer, and all kinds of musick, ye fall down and worship the golden image that Nebuchadnezzar the king had set up: And whoso falleth not down and worshippeth shall the same hour be cast into the midst of a burning fiery furnace." Please read the whole chapter of Daniel 3 and watch how this story unfolds. The term "worship" is used eleven times in this chapter and is amazingly similar to Revelation 13.

Revelation 12:17 says, "The dragon was wroth with the woman, and went to make war with the remnant of her seed, which keep the commandments of God and the testimony of Jesus Christ." This woman represents God's church. He has always

Ambushed in CHURCH?

had a remnant people. A remnant is something that still remains. The devil has always tried to stamp out the remnant, but the blood of martyrs was seed that grew and spread the gospel around the world.

We might think Sunday legislation could never happen in America. However, to stop the moral decay we see coming from so many factions and in order to turn the country back to God and a higher standard of morality, church and state will once again unite and that will usher in Sunday legislation in compliance with the moral majority.

As a Christian, I have to agree with much of what the moral majority stands for: getting prayer back in our schools, stopping abortions, stopping crime and the filth coming out of Hollywood, stopping the drug traffic, etc. It would seem to be a logical way to turn the country back to God. However, on the heels of these good things comes the enforcement of Sunday worship.

The little horn seems to have been in remission the last couple of hundred years. Don't be fooled. Revelation 17:8 says: "They that dwell on the earth shall wonder ... when they behold the beast that was, and is not, and yet is."

The irony is that those who were protesting against the atrocities of the Catholic Church and fleeing for their lives (the Protestants) have stopped protesting and in many ways are ready to join hands on certain beliefs they hold in common, mainly the observance of Sunday. Organizations like the religious coalition founded by Pat Robertson are carrying out the work

Chapter II

of this beast that was and is not, yet is. This is the beast John saw coming up out of the sea.

About the time of the fall of the papal power in 1798 A.D. a new nation was being formed, and this leads us to the second beast John sees in Revelation chapter 13. Look at verse 11. John says, "I beheld another beast coming up out of the earth." Remember, a beast represents kingdoms or nations. Also remember the first beast came up in the populated part of the world. Therefore one coming up out of the earth would mean the opposite: An unpopulated place or wilderness. Verse 11 continues. John says this beast "had two horns like a lamb." Notice there are no crowns on these horns. This nation is not governed by a king. A lamb is a gentle animal. What nation comes to power at the same time as the first beast goes down? What nation has been a lamb-like nation? A kind and gentle nation who sends aid to other nations all over the world? What nation has both civil and religious liberty and freedom, which is symbolized by the two horns? It would be the United States of America.

However, verse 11 doesn't end there: "And he spake like a dragon." Something is going to change in America before it's over. Verse 12 goes on to say, "He exerciseth all the power of the first beast before him and causeth the earth and them which dwell therein to worship the first beast, whose deadly wound was healed." Verse 14 says it "deceiveth them that dwell on the earth by the means of those miracles which he had power to do in the sight of the beast; saying to them that dwell on the earth, that they should make an image to the beast, which had the wound by the sword, and did live." Verse 15 says: "And he had power to give life unto the image of the beast, that the image of the beast should both speak and cause as many as would not worship the image to the beast should be killed."

Apostate Protestantism forms an image (a reflection of the first beast) by demanding worship. I wish this could never happen in America, but the Bible has never been wrong because it is God's word. When Protestants join hands with the Church of Rome, agreeing on points they hold in common, accompanied by undeniable miracles, then the union of the dragon, the beast, and the false prophet is formed as foretold in Revelation 16:13–14: "And I saw three unclean spirits like frogs come out of the mouth of the dragon, and out of the mouth of the beast, and out of the mouth of the false prophet. For they are the spirits of devils, working miracles, which go forth unto the kings of the earth and of the whole world, to gather them to the battle of that great day of God Almighty."

We don't know all the details that bring it together, but I believe the final movements will be rapid. The turning point may be a total economic collapse; or it may be terrorist attack; or a nuclear or natural disaster; maybe a computer chip will bring in a new

Chapter II

world order. But the real issue will be over worship, the real mark of the beast comes to fruition when its mark—which in their own words is Sunday—is legislated and put in force. When world leaders lose control and turn to religious leaders, church and state will once again unite and the part of the Constitution of our great nation which guarantees freedom of religion will be changed. The government of this beautiful country will speak with a different voice than that of a lamb.

The first book of the Bible, Genesis, tells of the Garden of Eden. Adam and Eve, our first parents, were free to eat from every tree. There was just one tree they were told not to eat the fruit of or they would die. That tree was a test of loyalty and love. Would they be true? Would they be faithful to their Creator? The choice was theirs. It was the only tree by the way that the serpent could tempt them from. They listened to the deceptive voice of the serpent, the most subtle beast of the field (Gen. 3:1).

Just before the Lord comes there is once again a test of loyalty and love. There is only one day He asks us to keep holy in honor of Him, our Creator and Redeemer. Will we be true to our God? Or listen to cunningly devised fables? Peter warns in 2 Peter 1:16: "For we have not followed cunningly devised fables, when we made known unto you the power and coming of our Lord Jesus Christ, but were eyewitnesses of his majesty." Verse 19 says: "We have also a more sure word of prophecy; whereunto ye do well that ye take heed." Jesus said in Matthew 15:9, "In vain do they worship me, teaching for doctrine the commandments of men."

> **Jesus said in Matthew 15:9,
> "In vain do they worship me, teaching for doctrine the commandments of men."**

Rome's sign of authority is the Sunday Sabbath. God's sign of authority is the seventh-day Sabbath. It has His seal on it. His name, title, and domain.

Long standing traditions are hard to break away from. Millions of good people go to church on Sunday because their parents did, and their grandparents did and so on back. And God does not condemn those sincere and precious ones. They are living according to the light they had been shown. However, when the truth is made known to an individual then, as Peter said in Acts 5:29, "we ought to obey God rather than men." It takes faith and courage to stand up and step out from long held beliefs.

When I was a little boy my mom and dad were Baptists. As my mom studied her Bible she discovered the truth about the Sabbath. It's mentioned over fifty times in the New Testament alone, and multiple times in the Old. The first day is mentioned eight times, and not once referring to worship. So she went to her Baptist minister and asked him about it. He told her, "Yes, the seventh day is the Sabbath of the Bible, but if I were to preach that I would lose my whole congregation." She politely thanked him, but never went back.

James 2:10 says, "For whosoever shall keep the whole law, and yet offend in one point, he is guilty of

Chapter II

all." My mom found a church that upholds all ten of God's commandments. It's the Seventh-day Adventist Church, a church that's often accused of being legalistic because of it. Again the only commandment under attack is the fourth commandment. If we see the Bible as a lot of "dos and don'ts" then we need to look to the cross. If the law could be broken, Jesus would not have had to die. Legalism all fades away in the light of the cross. Jesus wants to take that law and place it where it really means something—in our hearts. In Hebrews 8:10 God says, "I will put my laws into their mind, and write them in their hearts: and I will be to them a God, and they shall be to me a people." When God's law is in our hearts the Sabbath as well as the other nine is no longer a burden, but a joy. As David says in Psalm 40:8, "I delight to do thy will, O my God. Thy law is within my heart."

    I plead with you, friend, to be honest in your heart, pray about this, look at the great prophecies of the Bible. Look at history. Be reasonable. Good, old common sense is a good thing. For example, does a true Christian think he or she will be a resident of heaven if they keep on stealing or killing, or committing adultery? Of course not. Well, the same would be true for the fourth commandment. We wouldn't keep on breaking that one either if we're heaven bound. Not after it becomes clear to us from God's word.

    In Washington, D.C. there is a wall. On that wall are the names of all those who gave their lives in Vietnam for our country. I love my country and as a Vietnam veteran I realize what a disgrace and dishonor it would be to our veterans and our country if someone was to blast a hole in that wall! Yet that is exactly what has been done to God's law, by cutting away and treading down the fourth commandment, the one with His name on it. What shame and reproach to Him who gave His life to save us all from sin! God's moral law is a wall of protection around us. If upheld and honored, how different our world would be! The enemy of God has blasted a hole in it, but God has a people that are called the repairers of the breach. They are Sabbath keepers. Isaiah 58:12–13 says, "And they that shall be of thee shall build the old waste places: thou shalt raise up the foundations of many generations, and thou shalt be called, The repairer of the breach. The restorer of paths to dwell in. If thou turn away thy foot from the sabbath, from doing thy pleasure on my holy day; and call the sabbath a delight, the holy of the Lord, honourable; and shalt honour him, not doing thine own ways, nor finding thine own pleasure, nor speaking thine own words."

    I hope what I have written here will be a window through which you can see a glimpse of one of the greatest deceptions the world has encountered. Like I said, the battle between Christ and Satan is for your soul. Even though the battle is still on, remember this: Jesus Christ won the war on Calvary. When from the cross He cried, "It's finished," salvation was made sure to all who believe on Him (John 3:16). The believer will hear His voice and follow Him wherever He shall lead.

Chapter II

I love Jesus my Savior. I love His Sabbath day which honors Him and will throughout eternity. Eternity? Yes, look at this: "And it shall come to pass, that from one new moon to another, and from one Sabbath to another, shall all flesh come to worship before me, saith the Lord" (Isa. 66:23).

Yes, there are some frightening things coming ahead. In Matthew 24:21 Jesus says, "For then shall be great tribulation, such as not since the beginning of the world to this time, no, nor ever shall be." Read the whole chapter of Matthew 24. It tells about false prophets, false christs, great signs and wonders, amazing deceptions that, if possible, would deceive the very elect. It talks about how it was in the days of Noah before the flood. Life was going on as usual. Noah's preaching was ignored for 120 years. Suddenly the flood came and took them all away. Only eight people were saved in that ark. Was that the moral majority?

Here's the good news. 1 John 4:18 says: "Perfect love casts out fear." Matthew 24 also talks about the second coming of Jesus. The hope of the faithful. When you get to heaven, ask the martyrs. Their love for Jesus and their desire to be with Him throughout eternity outweighed their fear of this temporary death. I want to love Him like that; I want to love Him so much that nothing in this world can come between me and my Savior. He took my place on the cross. He took my nails in His hands and feet. He took my crown of thorns and offers me a crown of life instead. My Friend that laid down His life for me is my King who's coming for me.

Ambushed in CHURCH?

My personal Savior can be yours too. If you're tired of the trials and struggles in this world, don't commit suicide. Turn your life over to Him, and get ready for the greatest event the world has ever seen: The second coming of Jesus, far outweighing the great deception of Satan. When that trumpet blows, the heavens will part as a scroll. Revelation 1:7 says "every eye shall see Him" coming down through that celestial corridor accompanied by millions of angels. It will be a straight shot to Heaven if you have the seal of God and are covered by His robe of righteousness. The only thing we can pack in is our character, and He will mold us to be like Him as we turn our lives over to Him each day. By beholding Him we become changed. It's time to stop beholding the corrupt things of this world, and look to Jesus the author and finisher of our faith. He will turn our hate to love, our fears and guilt to peace.

As I was leaving Vietnam, they got together a little band at the base called Bear Cat. That was the only homecoming I had. But it's going to be different this time. What a band there will be! What shouts of victory will be heard! I want to meet you there. Our song will be a song of redemption and together, the saints of all the ages, will praise God and give Him the glory as He says, "Welcome home, soldiers of the cross."

CHAPTER III

As I ripped open a bandage and started to place it over a sucking chest wound, someone behind me yelled, "Forget it! He's gone! Move on to the next one." Glancing down, I saw that the blood had stopped sucking in and out, and the man's breath had ceased. Gone! Over 58,000 American soldiers during the Vietnam war gone. Gone where? Gone into body bags and sent home to loved ones to be buried around the country.

What happens to a person when they die? I mean, what really happens? Deception is a terrible thing, especially when it concerns life and death, because precious souls are at stake for eternity. So let's talk straight about the other great deception the world has ever seen, a deception that is also taught and preached in the majority of churches. Again, I will use the Bible and some plain common sense. Thankfully, the Bible is so clear on this subject it leaves no room

Ambushed in CHURCH?

for doubt. So, as it says in Isaiah 1:18, "Come now and let us reason together" saith the Lord.

The majority of Christian religions teach that if you're a good person you go straight to heaven when you die. I do not mean to be disrespectful at all, but the Bible just does not teach that. In fact, Solomon, the wisest man that ever lived, wrote these words in Ecclesiastes 9:5: "The living know that they shall die, but the dead know not anything."

Jesus Christ Himself gives us a tremendously clear description of what death is. It's found in the New Testament book of John, the eleventh chapter. It's the story of Lazarus. Lazarus was a close and dear friend of Jesus. If you read the account you will see where Lazarus had gotten sick and died. In John 11:3 it tells us that Lazarus' sisters, Mary and Martha, sent a message to Jesus saying, "The one you love is sick."

They must have thought, "He has healed so many, surely He will come and heal our brother." However, Jesus did something unexpected. Verse 6 says He stayed where He was for two days. Then, in verse 11, speaking to His disciples He said: "Our friend Lazarus sleepeth; but I go, that I may wake him out of sleep."

Now let's read verses 12–14: "Then said His disciples, Lord if he sleep, he shall do well. Howbeit Jesus spake of his death: but they thought that He had spoken of taking a rest in sleep. Then said Jesus unto them plainly, Lazarus is dead."

It can't get much plainer. It's obvious that the Lord is associating death to the unconscious state

Chapter III

of being asleep. When you're sound asleep you don't know anything going on around you. Verse 17 tells us that when Jesus arrived at Bethany, Lazarus had been dead for four days already. His sisters and friends were in mourning and in verse 21 Martha said, "Lord, if thou hadst been here my brother had not died." Now, in verse 25 Jesus said to her, "I am the resurrection, and the life; he that believeth in me, though he were dead, yet shall he live."

Please take your Bible and follow this story. In verse 41 Jesus lifts His eyes and prays to His Father, then He cries with a loud voice, "Lazarus. Come forth!" Look what happens. Verse 44 says: "He that was dead came forth, bound hand and foot with graveclothes: and his face was bound about with a napkin. Jesus saith unto them, Loose him and let him go."

Notice this good man Lazarus did not come down from heaven. He came forth from the grave where they had laid him, still wrapped in the customary burial cloths. That is what the resurrection is all about. When Jesus comes at the end of this world He will call forth from the grave those who have gone to sleep trusting and believing in Him. He will cut them loose from the grave that held them. Death can't keep them in the ground when He that is the resurrection and the life calls them.

There is so much deception on this subject of death. Please turn the pages in your Bible again to 1 Thessalonians 4. Look at what the apostle Paul says here beginning with verse 13:

Ambushed in CHURCH?

But I would not have you to be ignorant, brethren, concerning them which are asleep, that ye sorrow not, even as others which have no hope. For if we believe that Jesus died and rose again, even so them also which sleep in Jesus will God bring with Him. For this we say unto you by the word of the Lord, that we which are alive and remain unto the coming of the Lord shall not prevent them which are asleep. For the Lord Himself shall descend from heaven with a shout, with the voice of the archangel, and with the trump of God; and the dead in Christ shall rise first: Then we which are alive and remain shall be caught up together with them in the clouds, to meet the Lord in the air: and so shall we ever be with the Lord. Wherefore comfort one another with these words (1 Thess. 4:13–18).

Notice when Christ comes the living and the dead go up together. What a comfort that is! What a God we have! Where have all the soldiers gone? Where have our loved ones gone that have passed away? Gone to sleep, kept safe in the care of a heavenly Father who watches over every grave. It just doesn't get any plainer. Just stop and think about it. A mother dies and goes to heaven leaving her little child behind. Or a little baby is snatched from its mother's arms in death. What heartache there would be

> *Where have all the soldiers gone? Where have our loved ones gone that have passed away?*

Chapter III

in Heaven if those who have died and gone to heaven and could look down and see the suffering their loved ones are going through here? How happy would heaven be? Heaven would be hell! It just makes sense that a loving God would let us go together. And that's exactly what the Bible teaches.

So, where did this great deception taught by so many ministers and theologians come from? We can trace it all the way back to the Garden of Eden. In Genesis chapter 3 the Lord told Adam and Eve they could eat of every tree of the Garden except for one, "lest you die." Look at verse 4: "The serpent said unto the woman, you shall not surely die." Immortality of the soul is a pagan institution and through his first lie, "you shall not surely die," Satan entered the church through yet another avenue.

Eve was deceived and because she didn't trust the word of God, Eve died. And so death passed from our first parents down to all their descendants. Adam and Eve fell for the first lie ever told on earth. Down through the ages Satan has mastered the art of this deception. Why is it so important to him? It is because it's a set up for his final act of illusion.

In Revelation 16:13–14 John sees in vision three unclean spirits. It says: "[They] come out of the mouth of the dragon [Satan], and out of the mouth of the beast [papacy], and out of the mouth of the false prophet [apostate Protestantism]. For they are spirits of devils, working miracles, which go forth unto the kings of the earth and of the whole world." Through this three-fold union of Satan, the papacy, and

Ambushed in CHURCH?

apostate Protestantism comes powerful deception.

The increase in spiritualism today is undeniable. The media is promoting life after death everywhere: TV, magazines, videos, books, etc. Books on near death experiences are in best-seller status. Interest in spiritualism is mounting with fortunetellers, tarot readings, psychics, palm readings, and mediums communicating with the dead. The sincere Christian would turn away from ghost and witches, etc. yet these are all part of this great deception. Paganism takes on many forms. The Catholic Church claims to send the dead to heaven or a place called purgatory. The majority of Protestant churches teach that you go to heaven when you die.

When this three-fold union of the dragon, beast, and false prophet join together, the deception will be almost overwhelming. In fact, without a knowledge of God's word, it will be overwhelming. This is why Paul said in 1 Thessalonians that he didn't want us to be ignorant concerning them which sleep. In Psalm 146:4 it says: "His breath goes forth, he returneth to his earth; in that very day his thoughts perish."

Now, suppose you have a loved one who has died, maybe a mom or dad, or a child. One night they appear to you and talk with you. They talk about things that only you and they would know. Or maybe they describe how beautiful heaven is, etc. Will you believe what you see and hear with your own eyes and ears? It would be mighty hard not to, wouldn't it? Many have experienced this and are convinced they have

Chapter III

seen their loved one. The question is, will you believe your senses or will you, by faith, trust in God's word? I'm talking about strong delusion here. Satan is able to impersonate anyone, and he does. He knows all about you, and he's a master of deception.

Revelation chapter 12 tells us there was a war in heaven. Look at verses 7 through 9: "And there was war in heaven; Michael and his angels fought against the dragon, and the dragon fought and his angels and prevailed not, neither was their place found anymore in heaven. And the great dragon was cast out, that old serpent called the Devil and Satan, which deceiveth the whole world. He was cast out into the earth, and his angels were cast out with him."

Lucifer had been an angel, loved greatly by Christ. The problem was he wanted to be worshipped like Christ. But Lucifer was a created being. He was not God. Jesus was God, the Creator. The Bible says in John 1:3 that all things were made by Him. He was part of the Godhead made up of the Father, the Son, and the Holy Spirit, known as the Trinity. It's interesting that this Lucifer has made his own trinity: the dragon, the beast, and the false prophet. It's obvious that because of the terrible jealousy he had for Christ, that he began a work of deception right there in heaven. He had deceived many of the angels into following him as their leader.

So we see here in Revelation 12:7–9 that Satan and his angels were cast out into the earth. So not only does he have evil angels, but the Bible tells us in 2 Peter 2:1–2 that there are false prophets and false teachers that follow after his lies, many innocently. Satan is the cause of all the suffering, heartache, and pain in this world. Many wonder why a God of love would allow him to continue his evil work for so long when He could snuff him out in a second.

Think about this for a moment. If God did the snuff job, then somewhere out there, there might always be a bit of a question if maybe Satan was right in accusing God of being unjust by throwing him out of Heaven. So God allows him to do his work of destruction on the earth until God's name and righteousness is vindicated before the universe forever. By the time Satan is through, there will never be a question throughout eternity of God's justice and truth. Revelation 15:3 says: "And they sing the song of Moses the servant of God, and the song of the Lamb, saying, 'Great and marvelous are Thy works, Lord God Almighty; just and true are Thy ways, thou King of saints.'"

By the time Satan is through, there will never be a question throughout eternity of God's justice and truth.

There are a lot of indicators that this war between Christ and Satan is about to end. Satan has been doing his work of destroying the earth and all mankind for over six thousand years. He knows his time is short. It says so in Revelation 12:12. Therefore the apostle Peter says in 1 Peter 5:8: "Be sober, and vigilant; because your adversary the devil, as a roaring lion, walketh about, seeking whom he may devour." You see, Satan's going down, but he will take all he can with him. He

Chapter III

has the masses under his control through many, many avenues such as drugs, sex, and violence. Now he is gunning for the Christians more than ever.

2 Thessalonians 2:9 indicates there will be powerful signs and lying wonders. I remind you again of the words of Christ in Matthew 24:24, "If it were possible, they shall deceive the very elect." I believe many deceptive miracles are on the horizon, supernatural manifestations that can't be explained by science. For example, you might see an image of Mary weeping or bleeding. Remember, Mary is also resting in the ground, waiting for that resurrection morning.

Any church or pastor, or priest that teaches the immortality of the soul is not teaching Bible truth. Here's how I know. 1 Timothy 6:15–16, speaking of Christ says: "Which in His times He shall shew, who is the blessed and only Potentate, the King of kings, and Lord of lords! Who only hath immortality." <u>Christ alone</u>. The only ones the Bible tells us that have gone to heaven are: Moses, Elijah, Enoch, and a certain group that came out of their graves after Christ's resurrection.

Again we see from the Bible where bodies asleep in death came forth from the graves. Here it is, Matthew 27:52–53: "And the graves were opened; and many bodies of the saints which slept arose, and came out of the graves after His resurrection, and went into the holy city, and appeared unto many."

Let's look at some of the reasons given for the teaching that you go to heaven when you die. In Luke 23:43 we see the thief on the cross asking

Ambushed in CHURCH?

Jesus to remember him when He comes into His kingdom and Jesus answers. "And Jesus said unto him, Verily I say unto thee, Today thou shalt be with me in paradise.'" However, John makes it clear that Jesus didn't go to heaven that day. That was Friday when Jesus died, and it was Sunday morning when Mary came to the sepulcher and saw the risen Lord. In John 20:17 Jesus said to her: "Touch me not, for I am not yet ascended to my father." Bible scholars who have studied the ancient manuscripts found that those early manuscripts had no punctuation. Punctuation was put in later. Now it all makes sense if we take the same line, "I say unto you today, you shall be with me in paradise." With the comma after the word "today" instead of before it, then Luke 23:43 is in harmony with John 20:17.

What about Colossians 2:5 where Paul says: "For though I be absent in the flesh, yet am I with you in the spirit."? Well, Paul is writing to the people of Colosse, so obviously he's alive. He's simply saying though he's absent physically he's with them in spirit, thinking of them, praying for them, etc. We often say the same thing. In 2 Corinthians 5:8 Paul is explaining about being absent from the body, present in the spirit. If we look at verses 3 and 4 Paul is describing death as a state of nakedness or unclothed. However he hopes to be translated without seeing death. He would like to be absent from this world and be with his Lord, however he is confident that if he dies eternal life will begin at the resurrection. To say otherwise would be in contradiction with all his

Chapter III

other statements concerning this subject.

In 2 Corinthians 12:2-3 it says: "I knew a man in Christ above fourteen years ago (whether in the body, I cannot tell: or whether out of the body, I cannot tell: God knoweth;) such an one caught up to the third heaven. And I knew such a man (whether in the body, or out of the body, I cannot tell God knoweth)." Paul was simply saying when he had seen that vision of paradise fourteen years earlier that he doesn't understand how he could be here physically and be able to see heaven in vision as though he was there. He simply makes the statement, "God knows."

The apostle understood very clearly when the change from mortal to immortal takes place at the resurrection. Please read 1 Thessalonians 4:13-18 again. After you have read that, take a look at 1 Corinthians 15:51-55:

> Behold, I shew you a mystery; We shall not all sleep, but we shall all be changed, in a moment, in the twinkling of an eye, at the last trump: for the trumpet shall sound, and the dead shall be raised incorruptible, and we shall be changed. For this corruptible must put on incorruption, and this mortal must put on immortality. So when this corruptible shall have put on incorruption, and this mortal shall have put on immortality, then shall be brought to pass the saying that is written, Death is swallowed up in victory. O death, where is thy sting? O grave, where is thy victory.

Ambushed in CHURCH?

Let me take you back to Genesis. In Genesis 2:7 it says: "And the Lord God formed man of the dust of the ground, and breathed into his nostrils the breath of life, and man became a living soul." The body and the breath make up the soul. If you take away the breath the soul ceases to be until God calls us forth at the resurrection and gives us back the breath of life, and restores our body.

One theory is that at the resurrection the person's spirit comes back and re-enters the body. Stop and think: if the spirit's doing well in heaven, why would it need to come back for that old body? It doesn't make sense. "Come now and let us reason together," says the Lord.

The Bible mentions soul 1600 times, not once mentioning immortal soul. It doesn't get any plainer, does it? Immortality of the soul does, however, make good sense to Satan's strategy. For example, if someone is down with depression, strung out on drugs, lost all hope and wants out, and that person has been taught, often right in church, that when you die you go to heaven. Then that person is likely to commit suicide to get out of this crazy world and on to a better place. Suicide is becoming more prevalent every day, and it's promoted to a large degree right in church by those teaching the immortality of the soul.

Suicide is becoming more prevalent every day, and it's promoted to a large degree right in church by those teaching the immortality of the soul.

Chapter III

Let's look at Luke 16, beginning with verse 19. Jesus tells a parable of the rich man and Lazarus (not the same Lazarus he raised from the dead). A parable, though not an actual happening, teaches vital truths. The Lord used many parables to help people understand. Therefore keep in mind this is a parable in a string of other parables in Luke 15 and 16.

In the parable, a beggar named Lazarus (Luke 16:20–22) dies and is carried by angels to Abraham's bosom, and the rich man dies and is tormented in hell. He talks to Abraham and asks him to send Lazarus to him with some water. First of all, the Bible gives no record of Abraham being in heaven. Second, there would not be communication going on between people in heaven and people in hell. It wouldn't make sense for God to have the saved in heaven be able to see and hear the lost suffering in hell. The parable is showing how the rich man had everything money could buy, but he was morally bankrupt. He represents those who fail to take advantage of opportunities in life for formation of character and doing good to fellow men. In Verses 28–31 of Luke 16 the rich man in the parable says he has five brethren and says if one went to them from the dead they will repent, but in verse 31 Abraham says in the parable that they wouldn't be persuaded though one rose from the dead.

A few weeks after this parable Jesus gave living proof of the truth taught in the parable when He raised his friend the real Lazarus from the dead. The Pharisees were not persuaded. Matthew 13:13 says: "Therefore speak I to them in parables: because they seeing see not; and hearing they hear not, neither do they understand."

We would do well to study the Bible by subject. Look up everything the Bible says on a given subject and you will arrive at the whole truth. Man is on dangerous ground when he takes one or two verses out of context and builds a whole doctrine on it, and then teaches it to others. A couple of good examples of this is in Ecclesiastes 12:7. It says: "Then shall the dust return to the earth as it was: and the spirit shall return unto God who gave it." According to Strong's Concordance, the Hebrew word for spirit is *rûwach* and it means breath, exhalation, air. Many believe this text means when the body dies the spirit goes back to God and lives on. The reality of what's said in this text is that when a person dies the body returns to dust and the breath of life returns to God or just plain ceases. Common sense says God is not up there sucking in everybody's breath when they exhale the last time. The body must be united to the breath of life (spirit) to make a soul.

> *It's a jungle of confusion and deceit out there, and millions have been ambushed right in church.*

It's a jungle of confusion and deceit out there, and millions have been ambushed right in church. It's time we geared up for combat. The gear's different this time because we're not fighting against flesh and blood. The Bible tells us what we need. Here it is in Ephesians 6:10–18:

Chapter III

Finally, my brethren, be strong in the Lord, and in the power of His might. Put on the whole armor of God, that ye may be able to stand against the wiles of the devil. For we wrestle not against flesh and blood, but against principalities, against powers, against the rulers of the darkness of this world, against spiritual wickedness in high places. Wherefore take unto you the whole armour of God, that ye may be able to withstand in the evil day, and having done all, to stand. Stand therefore, having your loins girt about with truth, and having on the breastplate of righteousness; And your feet shod with the preparation of the gospel of peace; Above all, taking the shield of faith, wherewith ye shall be able to quench all the fiery darts of the wicked. And take the helmet of salvation, and the sword of the Spirit, which is the word of God: Praying always with all prayer and supplication in the Spirit, and watching thereunto with all perseverance and supplication for all saints (Eph. 6:10–18).

We can't fight against spiritual wickedness in high places, but Jesus can. And we can follow Him into battle, standing for truth with the shield of faith and the helmet of salvation.

I believe the Bible is the word of God and He keeps His word. I'm excited about His soon return. As we see life intensifying in the world and everything spinning out of control, it is of utmost importance that we understand within the wonderful gospel of salvation

Ambushed in CHURCH?

God also gives us information and warning that if heeded will keep us from being deceived.

The Bible is full of wonderful promises. Here are a few of my favorites: John 14:1–3: "Let not your heart be troubled: ye believe in God, believe also in Me. In My Father's house are many mansions: if it were not so, I would have told you. I go to prepare a place for you. And if I go and prepare a place for you, I will come again, and receive you unto myself, that where I am, there ye may be also."

Hebrews 7:25: "Wherefore He is able also to save them to the uttermost that come unto God by Him, seeing He ever liveth to make intercession for them."

2 Corinthians 12:9: "And He said unto me, My grace is sufficient for thee: for My strength is made perfect in weakness. Most gladly therefore will I rather glory in my infirmities, that the power of Christ may rest upon me."

Acts 4:12: "Neither is there salvation in any other: for there is none other name under heaven given among men, whereby we must be saved.

John 3:16: "For God so loved the world that He gave His only begotten Son, that whosoever believeth in Him should not perish but have everlasting life."

1 John 1:9: "If we confess our sins, He is faithful and just to forgive us our sins, and to cleanse us from all unrighteousness."

Romans 6:23: "For the wages of sin is death; but the gift of God is eternal life through Jesus Christ our Lord."

Ephesians 2:8: "For by grace are ye saved through faith; and that not of yourselves: it is the gift of God."

Chapter III

And finally, Revelation 21:1–5: "And I saw a new heaven and a new earth; for the first heaven and the first earth were passed away; and there was no more sea. And I John saw the holy city, new Jerusalem, coming down from God out of heaven, prepared as a bride adorned for her husband. And I heard a great voice out of heaven saying, Behold, the tabernacle of God is with men, and He will dwell with them, and they shall be His people, and God Himself shall be with them, and be their God. And God shall wipe away all tears from their eyes; and there shall be no more death, neither sorrow, nor crying, neither shall there be any more pain: for the former things are passed away. And He that sat upon the throne said, Behold, I make all things new. And He said unto me. Write: for these words are true and faithful."

Yes, Jesus is coming again and this time, my comrade, we will hear the words, *"Welcome Home."* I still remember as the big commercial jet with 270 replacement troops on board was coming down on the landing strip, the pilot's voice came over the intercom saying, "Good luck boys. I'll be back in one year to pick you up." I never forgot those words. I remembered them through over 200 enemy attacks. Just as that pilot said he would be back for me, Jesus Christ said He would be back for us! That's a promise of the God of Heaven that we can hold onto no matter how bad it gets.

This was the plan, remember? It was actually the plan before the world was even made. Let me touch on a few verses from 1 Peter 1:18–20. It says: "For as much as you know that you were not redeemed with

Ambushed in CHURCH?

corruptible things, or silver or gold. ... But with the precious blood of Christ, as of a lamb without blemish and without spot. Who verily was ordained before the foundation of the world."

When the Godhead made the decision to create this planet, Jesus volunteered that, if sin should arise, He would come and save His people that He would create. His children. You and me. Take some time and think about the chance He took for you. You see, during those thirty-three years that He lived among us, if He had committed one wrong act, one sin, He would have been eternally lost and separated from His Father, along with the rest of us. 1 John 3:4 says that "sin is the transgression of the law" and the law of God cannot be broken. It's who He is: His attributes, His character, His righteousness. Now, think about the cost. The price He paid for your salvation. He put it all on the line. All of heaven. His Father, Holy Spirit, angels. He gave everything to save you, and sealed the deal with His blood.

I once caught a glimpse of someone giving all. During the TET offensive of 1968 the village of Mỳ-Tho in the Mekong Delta was over run. During the night I was caught in the open under heavy enemy fire. Lying on the ground beside me was a little mama-san. This lady was severely wounded and dying. As I knelt beside her and put my helmet on her head, the shrapnel was smacking the ground all around us. As I took off my flack vest and laid it over her chest area I noticed in the light of a red flare she was nursing a baby on each breast. I couldn't speak her

Chapter III

language, but I could read it in her eyes. "I'm giving all I have. Please save my babies." I will never forget those eyes.

I plead with you my brother, my sister, to keep your eyes upon Jesus. Study His word and you won't be deceived by the beast and its false Sabbath, or the false doctrines so blatantly bombarding the Christian world. As the Catholic Church is calling all churches to come home to the mother church, God is calling the faithful to come out of her

Here it is: God's final call to you found in Revelation 18:4, "Come out of her my people." Here is that woman riding on the scarlet-colored beast, the mother of harlots, Babylon, the confusion of the centuries, the false doctrine that Satan has set up. Let's read it. Revelation 18:1–4:

> *Here it is: God's final call to you found in Revelation 18:4, "Come out of her my people."*

> And after these things I saw another angel come down from heaven, having great power; and the earth was lightened with his glory. And he cried mightily with a strong voice, saying, Babylon the great is fallen, is fallen, and is become the habitation of devils, and the hold of every foul spirit, and a cage of every unclean and hateful bird. For all nations have drunk of the wine of the wrath of her fornication, and the kings of the earth have committed fornication with her, and the merchants of the earth are waxed rich through the abundance

Ambushed in CHURCH?

of her delicacies. And I heard another voice from heaven, saying, Come out of her, my people, that ye be not partakers of her sins, and that ye receive not of her plagues.

We have this hope that soon the lies, the injustices, the wars, the pain and suffering the devil has caused in this world will end. And it's not just a hope. It's a promise. Our tour of duty is almost over. One day very soon our Heavenly Father is going to look into the eyes of His Son and say, "It's time. Go and bring My children home!"

I want to go home! I want to go home! Don't you? Be faithful friend, I want to see you there.

P.S. For further study about the good news of Salvation please take advantage of the Bible studies offered in the back of this book.

BIBLIOGRAPHY

Ancestor Search. http://www.searchforancestors.com/utility/gregorian.html.

Barry, J.B. *The History of the Decline and Fall of Roman Empire*, Vol 2.

Binney, Amos. *Methodist Theological Compendium, The.* 1902 Ed.

Boak, Arthur E.R. *A History of Rome.* New York: Macmillan Co. 1921.

Catholic World. Mar. 1894.

Christian at Work, The. Apr. 1883.

Dale, R.W. *The Ten Commandments.* London: Hodder and Stoughton, 1891.

Ambushed in CHURCH?

Domville, Sir William. *The Sabbath or An Examination of the Six Texts.* London: Chapman and Hall, 1849.

Ferraris, Lucius. Papa. Promota Bibliotheca. Vol. 6. Part 2.

Hisacox, Dr. Edward T. "Report of sermon at the Baptist Ministers Convention". *New York Examiner.* Nov. 16, 1893.

Melanchthon, Philipp. The Augsburg Confession. June 1530.

O'Brien, John A. Ph.D. *The Faith of Millions.* Huntington: Our Sunday Visitor. 1938.

"Sabbath Observance." *The Catholic Record.* 1 Sept. 1923. Print.

Segun, Louis Gaston. *Plain Talk about the Protestantism of Today.* Boston: Patrick Donahoe. 1868. Print.

The Holy Bible, Authorized King James Version. Nashville: Holman Bible Publishers. 1982.

"The Question Box." *The Catholic Universe Bulletin.* 1 Aug 1942.

Thomas, C.F, Chancellor of Cardinal Gibbons. Letter. 28 Oct. 1895.

I married this author the year after he returned from Vietnam. It wasn't long before he began having what we later learned were night terrors and he stopped sleeping. It was a tough time for him. This book is a culmination of his years of seeking and learning. No words are meant to hurt any person nor denigrate anyone's belief system. He writes as he has discovered through much prayer and study and only wishes to help other Vietnam veterans and the rest of us learn as he has learned.

He served in the Vietnam theatre in 1967–1968 as a combat medic. The war had reached a boiling point as evidenced by anyone who served there during the Tet Offensive of 1968. He knows what it is like to be under attack from both the enemy as well as for his faith in God.

Well aware that what he has written here will likely bring him under attack again, he is still determined to make known the truths that have been lost sight of through the years. It may surprise many to learn of the deceptions that are believed and taught in churches by many with sincere hearts. He was dedicated to saving lives in Vietnam and he is dedicated to saving souls now from the deceptions that have infiltrated the church.

He praises God for the many times his life was spared and for each new day to live.

His prayer each day is that the Lord will take the words of an unprofessional writer and make known the simple truths of God's Word to every reader of this book.

We invite you to view the complete
selection of titles we publish at:

www.TEACHServices.com

Scan with your mobile device to go directly to our website.

Please write or email us your praises, reactions, or thoughts about this or any other book we publish at:

P.O. Box 954
Ringgold, GA 30736

info@TEACHServices.com

TEACH Services, Inc., titles may be purchased in bulk for educational, business, fund-raising, or sales promotional use.
For information, please e-mail:

BulkSales@TEACHServices.com

Finally, if you are interested in seeing your own book in print, please contact us at

publishing@TEACHServices.com

We would be happy to review your manuscript for free.

HAVE QUESTIONS?

FIND ANSWERS

Can God be trusted? Is there hope for our planet? What must we do to have eternal life? Why does God allow suffering? Can we understand Bible prophecy? Find answers to these and other questions—straight from the Bible!

The **It Is Written Bible Study Guides** feature 25 lessons that use a simple fill-in-the-blank format, with an answer key included. The complete set is available for only $9.99 (plus shipping).

To order, please call toll-free 1-888-664-5573. Or order online from our website at **www.itiswritten.com/biblestudy**.

www.itiswritten.com
facebook.com/itiswritten
twitter.com/itiswritten

© 2014 It Is Written Television. All rights reserved.

www.ingramcontent.com/pod-product-compliance
Lightning Source LLC
Chambersburg PA
CBHW070545170426
43200CB00011B/2566